COLORING BOOK

COVER OF THIS COLORING BOOK HAS BEEN
DESIGNED USING RESOURCES FROM FREEPIK.COM

COLOR TEST PAGE

© SILLY GROWN PRESS
ALL RIGHTS RESERVED

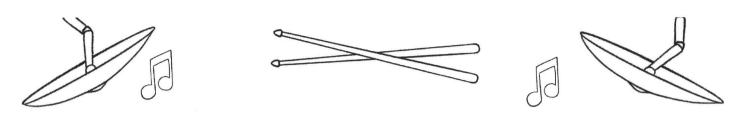

DRUMMERS

GONNA

DRUM

IF YOU LIKED THIS COLORING BOOK CONSIDER LEAVING A REVIEW ON AMAZON

ALSO IF YOU ARE INTERESTED IN MORE FUNNY COLORING BOOKS FOR ADULTS
BE SURE TO CHECK OUT:
,,SILLY GROWN PRESS"
ON AMAZON

Printed in Great Britain
by Amazon